RIPPLES FROM CARCOSA

THREE SCENARIOS EXPLORING HASTUR, CARCOSA, & THE KING IN YELLOW

Written by **Oscar Rios**

Edited and Developed by **Mike Mason**

Art Direction and Interior Layout by **Meghan McLean**

Cover Layout by **Charlie Krank**

Interior Art by **Bradley McDevitt, Marco Morte,** and **Erik York**

Cover Art by **Jan Pospíšil**

Maps by **Gill Pearce** and **Steff Worthington**

Table of Contents

Dedication

This book is dedicated to Richard Watts, my friend, my mentor, and the classiest man I know. I wrote *Ripples From Carcosa* when I was a new author struggling to find my feet. I was inspired by several classic *Call of Cthulhu* scenarios, but primarily by "Tatterdemalion", written by Richard Watts. I discovered that Richard and I were both members of the same message board so I did what any fan-boy would do. I contacted him, told him how he'd inspired me to write the *Ripples From Carcosa*. Richard Watts not only answered my note but he offered to review the manuscript before I submitted it. I was thrilled and sent it over. Several days later I got a lengthy reply; four paragraphs on why he liked it, followed by four pages listing everything wrong with it and pointed out all the missed opportunities. Most importantly he explained ways I could fix every single thing he felt needed work. I got back to work, going step by step, following his instructions like a treasure map. I learned more about the art of writing from that single email than I ever had in school. This man, a total stranger, helped me. He didn't have to and I am not sure why, but he did. For that I am eternally grateful. So to Richard Watts, *Thank You*.

Ripples From Carcosa is published by Chaosium Inc.

Ripples From Carcosa is copyright as a whole © 2014 by Chaosium Inc.; all rights reserved.
Text is copyright © 2014 by Oscar Rios.

This adventure pack is best used with the roleplaying game *Call of Cthulhu*, available separately. *Call of Cthulhu*®
is the registered trademark of Chaosium Inc. Find more Chaosium Inc. products at **www.chaosium.com**

Follow Chaosium on Twitter @Chaosium_Inc

Similarities between characters in *Ripples From Carcosa* and persons living or dead are strictly coincidental.

The reproduction of material from within this book for the purposes of personal or corporate profit, by
photographic, electronic, or other methods of retrieval, is prohibited.

Address questions and comments concerning this book to

Chaosium Inc.
22568 Mission Boulevard #423
Hayward CA 94541-5116

Chaosium publication 23134. Published in August 2014.

ISBN/EAN: 9781568824017

Printed in the United States.

Introduction

*"O do not seek to learn or even ask,
What horror hides behind…The Pallid Mask!"*

~Lin Carter, "Litany to Hastur"

Of all the varied and mysterious Great Old Ones of the Cthulhu Mythos, few ensnare the imagination as easily as Hastur. The image of the silent, deserted city beside a dark, foreboding lake where sinister things lurk is one that stays with the reader. Many of us have walked the twisting streets of that dead alien city in our minds, finding our way into the tall towers to stand before an ancient throne. There sits the King in Yellow, the Lord of Carcosa, who gazes at us from behind his Pallid Mask. It is a journey many of us have taken, whether alone in our dreams or around a table rolling dice with our friends. It is a journey we are about to take again.

Many of us have a favorite writer or musician who spiraled into insanity before taking their own life; artists, poets, dreamers, and madmen feel the hand of the Great Old Ones most clearly. The line between creative genius and abject madness is a thin one. Hastur is the gray area where those two spheres overlap. His play, *The King in Yellow*, has long been one of the most popular of all Mythos Tomes. His triskelion Yellow Sign is a symbol nearly as recognizable as the Elder Sign.

Ripples from Carcosa seeks to expand upon the mythology of "He Who Should Not Be Named" and it gathers much of the varied material on Hastur into one place. The first chapter reviews The Great Old One Hastur and his various avatar forms. It examines the Yellow Sign, the play *The King in Yellow*, the Mythos tome of the same name, and the effects these things have on the human mind. While far from being a comprehensive archive of all that is written on the topic, it should answer the most common questions and provide keepers with a central resource.

Next within these pages is a trio of adventures pitting investigators against Hastur and his human worshippers. These scenarios can be played as stand-alone adventures or as a linked campaign

called "Ripples from Carcosa." Investigators are provided for each scenario, but keepers should feel free to allow their players to use their own investigators if they so choose.

The first scenario, entitled "Adventus Regis," takes place during the time of the Roman Empire and uses the *Cthulhu Invictus* setting. The second scenario is called "Herald to the Yellow King;" its events occur during the Dark Ages. This scenario, naturally, utilizes the *Cthulhu Dark Ages* setting. The keeper may it useful to access these Chaosium titles. The final chapter of the trilogy is called "Heir to Carcosa;" it's set in mankind's near future. It uses a possible "End Time" setting (one as detailed in the Chaosium monograph of the same name).

Following the first two scenarios is information on the Great Old One Hastur and his cults during the *Cthulhu Invictus* and *Cthulhu Dark Ages* eras. Keepers who wish to expand upon those scenarios can make use of this source material to present further investigation of He Who Should Not Be Named during those historical periods. "The Servants of the Yellow Sign," the cult of Hastur within Herculaneum, is presented for the *Cthulhu Invictus* setting. Likewise a cult group called the "Court of the Last King," is a 10th century Hastur Cult operating in France, and detailed for the *Cthulhu Dark Ages* setting. Before the final scenario, material is included detailing a futuristic society: a coalition of humans and aliens living and hiding in our solar system's asteroid belt. This is for use during the "End Time" setting, a period set in a future where mankind has lost the Earth to the forces of the Mythos. This last secretive group is not a cult worshiping Hastur but one dedicated to fighting against such forces.

RIPPLES FROM CARCOSA

Playing the scenarios as a campaign:

*"Every Christmas it's the same.
I always end up playing a shepherd."*

~ Shermie, *A Charlie Brown Christmas*

2

Together Again and Again

As each scenario takes place roughly one thousand years apart, one might wonder how they can be played as a linked campaign. The eighteen pre-generated investigators included across the trilogy are reincarnations of the same six sets of consciousness. On their first encounter with Hastur in the Roman Era they are marked, branded somehow, and forever after tied to the Great Old One throughout eternity. Once every millennium they are drawn together and once again forced to confront the horror and madness of He Who Should Not Be Named.

From era to era the reincarnated investigators share certain similarities. From lifetime to lifetime these consciousnesses fall back into the patterns and the professions they are best suited for. This should help promote the feeling that they are somehow trapped by fate. The fact that these investigators are continually drawn together into conflict with the various manifestations of Hastur should also reinforce this.

The players may view their investigators as cursed, being doomed to lead the same life over and over, trapped and drawn into encounters with The Great Old One Hastur. They might view themselves as chosen defenders of humanity, heroes who band together, lifetime after lifetime, to thwart the aims of He Who Should Not Be Named. The reason for this, if any, is left up to the individual keeper.

Hastur Lore

All Mythos-related events in *Ripples from Carcosa* are directly tied to Hastur. Therefore, investigators learn little about the overall Cthulhu Mythos but a great deal of specific information about He Who Should Not Be Named. To reflect this knowledge keepers are encouraged to use a skill called Hastur Lore.

The Hastur Lore skill is much like the Cthulhu Mythos skill and directly tied to it. It can be used to uncover information about Hastur, his avatar forms, Carcosa, the Yellow Sign, the Mythos races connected with the Great Old One, etc. For every single percentile point of Cthulhu Mythos traditionally earned in *Ripples from Carcosa*, investigators gain +3% in their Hastur Lore skill. For example: An investigator reads a copy of *The King In Yellow* in its original French. The investigator gains 6 percentiles of Cthulhu Mythos and also 18 percentiles of Hastur Lore.

Unlike Cthulhu Mythos, an investigator's Hastur Lore skill has no effect on their maximum Sanity value. The Cthulhu Mythos skill remains unchanged with regards to an investigator's possible Sanity loss. Hastur Lore doesn't get checked for advancement after a successful use. The only way for an investigator to gain points in Hastur Lore is by increasing their knowledge of and exposure to Hastur.

Certain encounters also earn the investigators Cthulhu Mythos and Hastur Lore skill points in this campaign. Not all knowledge comes from research; some is gained from experience. Below is a list of things that increase an investigator's Hastur Lore skill. Keepers are encouraged to create new ones on the fly as investigators learn more and more about their powerful and mysterious nemesis.

Experience	Cthulhu Mythos %/ Hastur Lore %
Seeing the Yellow Sign for the first time.	1% / 3%
Encountering a servitor race of Hastur.	2% / 6%
View city of Carcosa or the Lake of Hali.	2% / 6%
Encountering a creature native to Carcosa.	3% / 9%
Visit and explore city of Carcosa.	4% / 12%
Viewing an avatar form of Hastur.	5% / 15%

Déjà Vu, the Yellow Sign, and Past Life Recollections

In the second and third scenarios of *Ripples from Carcosa* the investigators can draw upon past-life experiences. The trigger for this ability is an investigator's initial exposure to the Yellow Sign. While a potent tool for causing and spreading insanity, the Sign also unlocks a psychic echo within the investigator's consciousness. The trauma this powerful and malevolent symbol causes to the investigators creates a scar upon them, which transcends the limits of their individual lifetimes.

What this means is that the points of Cthulhu Mythos and Hastur Lore investigators acquire in one scenario can be accessed and improved on during the following adventures. Thus an investigator's Cthulhu Mythos skill grows and is carried over throughout each reincarnation. For example: Videric, a woodsman in "Herald of the Yellow King," sees the Yellow Sign for the first time. After making his Sanity check he suddenly gains 9% in Cthulhu Mythos and 27% of Hastur Lore. These are points he acquired in his previous life as Marcius, a thief who encountered Hastur in the time of the Roman Empire during the scenario "Adventis Regis." Investigators only have access to these points after, and only if, they view the Yellow Sign. Otherwise these memories remain forever locked away.

In "Herald of the Yellow King" these past-life memories manifest as moments of déjà vu or powerful intuitive feelings. The investigators "know" things without any logical way of determining precisely how. They also possess vague feelings of a certain familiarity, as if all this has somehow happened before.

"HERALD OF THE YELLOW KING," DARK AGES EXAMPLE:

Lady Charlotte: "What, I ask thee, is that?"

Redwald, after making a successful Hastur Lore roll: "'Tis the 'Yellow Sign,' my Lady. It bringeth the curse of madness, and 'tis mark of a demon prince of madness."

Lady Charlotte: "How is it that you know this, good sir?"

Redwald: "I have no idea how I know this thing, my lady. But I assure you from the depths of my immortal soul that is the truth!"

Investigators who meet horrible ends, experienced powerful personal loss, or are driven insane during "Adventis Regis" feel these impulses more strongly, as their trauma is more profound. For Example: An investigator is driven insane by the Yellow Sign in "Adventis Regis." They are then reincarnated and see the Yellow Sign again, during the Dark Ages, in "Herald of the Yellow King." The player of this investigator makes a successful Hastur Lore roll and not only knows what the Yellow Sign is but also receives intuitive feelings that the symbol is very dangerous. They realize something bad happened to them the last time they encountered this symbol, but exactly what occurred and when that was is a mystery to them.

In "Heir to Carcosa" such feelings are intensified. This reflects the greater number of points so far accumulated from two separate investigations. Instead of feeling déjà vu and flashes of intuition, investigators receive visions of their past lives racing through their minds. After seeing the Yellow Sign, investigators in this era universally feel that not only have they all been together and through something similar before, but that it may have happened more than once.

Keepers should play such flashbacks as if they are attacks of post-traumatic stress disorder. The visions should be vivid and realistic memories of terrifying past events. Investigators who experience this should be momentarily stunned, lost in the memory for a moment before snapping back to reality. Each such "memory flash" causes the loss of 1 Sanity point.

"HEIR TO CARCOSA," END TIMES EXAMPLE:

Martin Smith: "What the hell was that thing?"

Andrew Fisk, after making a successful Hastur Lore roll and losing 1 point of Sanity: "It's a byakhee. They can survive in a vacuum and fly through space. They're very dangerous up close."

Martin Smith: "Yeah… okay…and you know this how?"

3

Andrew Fisk: "'Cause one of them almost killed me once. Not now, but once, a long time ago. You're gonna think I'm crazy, but I think you were there too."

Damien Gunn, after overhearing this and making a successful Hastur Lore roll and also losing 1 point of Sanity: "Was I there too, maybe in Roman-style armor with a sword?"

Andrew Fisk: "Yeah, you were! What the hell is going on?"

Keepers can have investigators experience nightmares with two or more of them experiencing the very same dream. This is actually a shared past-life experience, which their unconscious minds are recollecting while they slumber. Such a shared dream could possibly give some clue to a problem the investigators are struggling with.

HEIR TO CARCOSA, SHARED DREAMS, END TIMES EXAMPLE:

Diana Everett: "You didn't sleep well either?"

Lola Voight: "No, I had a nightmare. We were all on Earth and it was snowing. Real snow, like on the old vids. It was cold; we were trying to get somewhere and this bridge…"

Diana Everett, interrupting: "It just kept stretching on and on! I had the same dream!"

Vincent Delgato, joining in after overhearing the exchange: "And then tentacles came out of the water. Yeah, I had the same dream too."

Diana Everett: "Okay, we can't all be going crazy."

And so we are ready to begin. The star Aldebaran is above the horizon, the mists are rising off the Lake of Hali, and He Who Should Not Be Named is lurking just offstage. I give you *Ripples From Carcosa*.

A Guide to Hastur, The Yellow Sign, and "The King In Yellow"

This chapter contains a compilation of various materials from several different sources. It is included here as an overview for keepers, who may be unfamiliar with the mythos surrounding Hastur. Think of this as a crash course in Hastur's fundamentals. It is far from complete, as the mythology surrounding He Who Should Not Be Named is both vast and complex. Three areas presented here are as follows:

- Hastur the Unspeakable and three of his avatar forms.
- The Yellow Sign and the effects it has upon the human mind.
- The book entitled *The King in Yellow* and the play of the same name.

The Lake of Hali, the dead city of Carcosa, and the various ways investigators can travel to and from these locations is not covered here. Such information, while interesting and important to Hastur's mythology, does not come into play in the three scenarios that make up the *Ripples from Carcosa* trilogy. Should keepers wish to learn more about the home domain of Hastur, some classic scenarios are strongly recommended. "Have You Seen the Yellow Sign" by Kevin A. Ross, from the book *The Great Old Ones*, and "Tatterdemalion" by Richard Watts and Penelope Love, from *Fatal Experiments* are both are excellent scenarios for anyone interested in the Great Old One, Hastur. Additionally, the campaign *Tatters of the King* by Tim Wiseman provides a wealth of information concerning Carcosa.

The Great Old One, Hastur The Unspeakable

The four entries here are the statistics for and description of Hastur and three of his avatar forms: The King In Yellow, The Feaster From Afar, and The Boneless One. These are taken directly from Chaosium's *Malleus Monstrorum*. The Boneless One is a manifestation of Hastur, however specific statistics

for it were never provided. As this particular avatar plays heavily in the climax of "Adventus Regis" game statistics have been created.

HASTUR THE UNSPEAKABLE, GREAT OLD ONE

"Utterly alien landscape… Foreground: a deep lake. Hali. In five minutes the water began to ripple where something rose. Facing inwards. A titanic aquatic being, tentacled. Octopoid, but far, far larger ten-twenty times larger than the giant Octopus apollyon of the west coast. What was its neck alone easily fifteen rods in diameter. Could not risk chance of seeing its face."

~August Derleth, "The Gable Window"

Hastur the Unspeakable dwells near the star Aldebaran in the constellation Taurus. He is connected with the mystic Lake of Hali, the Yellow Sign, and Carcosa, as well as the things that dwell therein. He may be connected in some way with the power of flight through space. His appearance is disputed. In a reported instance of possession by Hastur, a corpse took on a bloated, scaly look, and the limbs became boneless and fluid. The things in the Lake of Hali look octopoid from a rear view and are related to Hastur. They also have unbearably horrible faces. Still, Hastur's appearance is largely up to the individual keeper. Hastur is served by the byakhee, an interstellar flying race.

CULT: The cult of Hastur is moderately common on Earth, and the abominable Tcho-Tcho people are reputedly among his worshipers, as are the Brothers of the Yellow Sign. Hastur's cult is particularly loathsome, and is more widely known of than belonged to. Worshipers refer to Hastur as "He Who Should

6

The King in Yellow Avatar

Not Be Named." This may be a misapprehension, stemming from his title, "The Unspeakable."

OTHER CHARACTERISTICS: Hastur is summonable only at night. When Hastur is present, each round three individuals within 20 yards of the horror must successfully Dodge or be grasped by Hastur and destroyed on the following round. Hastur does not normally attack friends or worshipers. He must always leave that portion of the Earth where the star Aldebaran has fallen below the horizon.

Hastur, He Who Should Not Be Named

STR 600	CON 1000	SIZ 500	INT 75
POW 175	DEX 150	APP --	EDU --
HP: 150	DB: +13D6	Build 14	Move 16 / 25 flying

Magic Points: 30

Attacks: 2

Whatever he is, Hastur has tentacles and claws among his appendages.

Fighting 100% (50/20), damage: death

Armor: 30-point thick, scaly, rubbery, baggy hide.

Spells: Brew Space Mead, All Contact and Call spells, Summon/Bind Byakhee, and others the keeper finds appropriate.

Sanity Loss: 1D10/1D100 Sanity points to see Hastur.

KING IN YELLOW, AVATAR OF HASTUR

"He stands in state upon the balcony. He has no face, and is twice as tall as a man. He wears pointed shoes under his tattered, fantastically colored robes, and a streamer of silk appears to fall from the pointed tip of his hood… At times he appears to be winged; at others, haloed."

– James Blish, "More Light"

The King in Yellow might also be human-seeming, clad in tattered yellow or parti-colored rags and wearing the Pallid Mask. The rags are extensions of the entity's flesh, while the mask covers horrible pseudopods that can attach to a target and drain the very life from them (POW). Above all, it possesses a loathsome plasticity of shape, able to stretch and change at will. This is the most frequently encountered avatar of Hastur.

CULT: Worshipers often are solitary madmen, artists, and poets, driven mad by reading the haunting play *The King In Yellow*, and inspired by its cruel beauty to create art that renders human experience meaningless. A special symbol, the Yellow Sign, is often stamped on surreptitious editions of the evil book. The Sign is a focus for madness, helping to warp the dreams of those who see it.

Gaze Of The Yellow King—Induces paroxysms of fear by staring at the target, costing the unfortunate 1D6 Sanity points per round while the King in Yellow focuses upon them (costing the King 3 magic points per round). To avoid the gaze for a round, the target must make an Extreme POW roll.

The King In Yellow, Throne Form

STR 125	CON 530	SIZ 70	INT 250
POW 175	DEX 135	APP --	EDU --
HP: 60	DB: +1D6	Build 2	Move 15*

Or can appear/disappear at will.

Magic Points: 35

Attacks: 1 gaze, 6 razor sharp tatters, or 1 face tentacle

Some say the King has a strange facial tentacle hidden behind his pallid mask with which he kisses his worshipers. Others say when he dances his tattered robes extend as pseudopodia, cutting those around him like razors.

Fighting 100% (50/20), damage by razor sharp tatters is 1D6 + DB +1D6 POW, or by face tentacle is 1D10 + DB + 1D10 POW per round while attached.

Gaze: Target must make Extreme POW roll to resist, special (see above).

Armor: None.

Spells: All Call, Contact spells, and others as the keeper desires.

Sanity Loss: With the Pallid Mask upon its 'face' there is no Sanity loss; however in any other form, or with the mask removed, it costs 1D3/1D10 Sanity points to see the King in Yellow.

FEASTER FROM AFAR, AVATAR OF HASTUR

"He felt it coming. The air grew frigid, as if it blew out of the black interstices of interstellar space... It glided down out of the icy sky like the final concentrated essence of all nonhuman horror. It was black, infinitely old, shriveled and humped like some kind of enormous air-borne monkey. A kind of iridescence played about it and its fixed blazing eyes were of no color known on earth... As it grew close to the knoll, it extended appendages, which resembled tentacles, tipped with knifelike talons."

–Joseph Payne Brennan,
"The Feaster from Afar"

CULT: This strange avatar of Hastur is little worshiped on Earth.

OTHER CHARACTERISTICS: Once called to Earth, The Feaster from Afar can return to the area of its summoning at will as long as Aldebaran is above the horizon and it is dark. Anyone with one or more points of Cthulhu Mythos in the area experiences vivid nightmares of being chased over an alien landscape by an unseen pursuer. The terror in these dreams is so intense that 0/1D2 Sanity points are lost each time the investigator has the nightmare.

The Feaster's approach is signaled by an icy wind that blows out of the night sky. This form of Hastur appears to be independent of attendant byakhee.

The Feaster attacks by puncturing holes in its victim's skull with its knife-like talons and draining out his or her brain. The bodies are left otherwise unharmed. Each round the Feaster can attack a single target with 2D10 talons. Each talon inflicts 1 hit point of damage and drains 5 points of INT. When a victim's INT is reduced to zero the Feaster turns its attention to another victim or departs. If a victim has any hit points left after his INT has reached zero, he or she does not immediately die; if the mindless individual is attached to life support devices within an hour or so of the attack, they may live. Such

The Feaster from Afar Avatar

mindless individuals live out their lives as vegetables, incapable of thought, movement, or sound.

The Feaster From Afar, Devourer of Brains.

STR 245	CON 525	SIZ 165	INT 50
POW 125	DEX 165	APP --	EDU --
HP: 69	DB: +4D6	Build 5	Move 16 / 30 Flying

Magic Points: 25

Attacks: 1 (4 talons on one target)

Fighting 90% (45/18), damage 1 point + 5 INT drain per talon.

Armor: 20 points of thick, wrinkled hide.

Spells: Any the keeper desires.

Sanity Loss: 1D8/1D20 Sanity points to see The Feaster from Afar.

THE BONELESS ONE, AVATAR OF HASTUR

"His appearance is disputed. In a reported instance of possession by Hastur, a corpse took on a bloated scaly look, and the limbs became boneless and fluid."

This manifestation of Hastur requires a living or recently-sacrificed human body to act as a vessel for the Great Old One's consciousness. The Boneless One is one of the most loathsome of all of Hastur's avatar forms. Slow and almost completely immobile, the Boneless One usually manifests on Earth for short times while the star Aldebaran is above the horizon. The corpse possessed by Hastur undergoes a startling physical change. It becomes elastic and boneless, bloating grotesquely while its skin becomes thicker and scaly. There is a 70% chance 3–8 (1D6+2) byakhee arrive 1–3 rounds after the avatar manifests, flying out of the cold depths of space ready to serve their master.

OTHER CHARACTERISTICS: The Boneless One is immune to fire, electricity, acid, and non-magical weapons. While this avatar form is the Great Old One's least powerful physically, it commands potent magical and psychic abilities. At will, the Boneless One can unleash a psychic wave of madness. This wave travels 50 feet per magic point expended, causing those within range to make a Sanity roll for 1D6/1D20.

The Boneless One, Avatar of Hastur

STR 75	CON 470	SIZ 80	INT 250
POW 175	DEX 75	APP --	EDU --
HP: 50	DB: 0	Build 0	Move 2

Magic Points: 35

Attacks: 1

Psychic wave (automatic),1D6/1D20 Sanity check.

Armor: 4 points of leathery skin; immune to fire, cold, electricity, acid, and non-magical weapons.

Spells: All Call, Contact, and Summon/Bind spells, plus any others the keeper wishes.

Sanity Loss: 1D6/1D10 Sanity points to see The Boneless One.

THE YELLOW SIGN

Purported to be the great seal of He Who Is Not To Be Named in his form as the King in Yellow, the Yellow Sign holds great interest and power to those learned in the ways of the occult. No one single pattern can be agreed upon as to the Sign's actual shape and design, with many claiming the Sign somehow changes in aspect whenever its master or His servants are near. For years the innocent and ignorant may pass the sign daily without re-

gard or knowledge of its significance; perhaps only in nightmares does the Sign register. However, once the Sign becomes 'active' the same person will see it where first they did not, and many times thereafter in places unsuspected. Any who has seen the Yellow Sign is considered blessed and chosen.

Perhaps working subliminally, the Yellow Sign is a focus for evil and madness, and essentially a token of high worship for Hastur's cults. Viewing the Yellow Sign causes 0/1D6 Sanity point loss. The Sign seems to swirl, shimmer and squirm, as if reaching for the onlooker. This effect takes but a moment; however, to the person affected it feels as if time has stood still. Those who lose sanity points from seeing the Yellow Sign are cursed; the next time they sleep they should make another Sanity roll and if failed, they suffer terrible nightmares concerning the King in Yellow, Carcosa and Hastur costing a further point of Sanity. Each time thereafter the person sleeps they should make a Sanity roll (0/1) and this is repeated each night until either they succeed in the Sanity roll or madness overtakes them.

THE KING IN YELLOW (THE BOOK)

One of the central themes of the Mythos connected with Hastur is the play *The King In Yellow*. The basic information on this book, in some of its numerous forms, is included for quick reference. Three new forms of this work appear in *Ripples from Carcosa*; a brief description of these works is also listed here. Greater details on these new incarnations of *The King In Yellow* are listed in the individual scenarios.

The Original French—This original edition was seized and destroyed by the Third Republic just after publication. The text is an ambiguous, dreamlike play, which opens readers to madness. Sanity loss 1D10; Cthulhu Mythos +2/+4 percentiles; Mythos Rating 18; average 1 week to study. Spells: None.

The King In Yellow English translation—The English edition is a thin black octavo volume across the front cover of which is embossed a large Yellow Sign. Sanity loss 1D10; Cthulhu Mythos +1/+4 percentiles; Mythos Rating 15; average 1 week to study. Spells: None.

Xanthic Folio—A set of ancient tablets found in China, said to be Elder Thing glyphs. This pre-

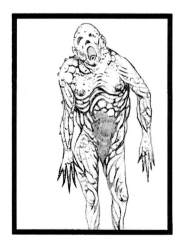

The Boneless One Avatar

human artifact details the King in Yellow and his court. Sanity loss 1D10; Cthulhu Mythos +3/+7 percentiles; Mythos Rating 30; average 7 weeks to study and comprehend. Spells: Create Time Warp.

Yellow Codices—A translation of the *Xanthic Folio*, often found in English and French. A French copy of the *Yellow Codices* was thought to be the inspiration for *The King In Yellow*. Copies of this work have circulated among groups of jaded artists and writers for years. Sanity Loss 1D8; Cthulhu Mythos +2/+6 percentiles; Mythos Rating 24; average 1 week to study and comprehend. Spells: None.

Alternate forms of The King In Yellow—In the three scenarios that make up *Ripples from Carcosa* the investigators won't encounter any of the above books. The story of The King In Yellow is presented in three new forms across each scenario of the trilogy:

- **"Adventus Regis"**—Here, during the time of the Roman Empire, an early version of the play *The King In Yellow* has just been written. It is entitled "Adventus Regis" (Arrival of the King), and the investigators have the opportunity to obtain a hastily-revised edition of the play.

- **"Herald of the Yellow King"**—In the Dark Ages chapter of the trilogy the investigators might listen to story of *The King In Yellow* as told by a wizened bard or read a brief version of the tale from an old priest's journal.

- **"Heir to Carcosa"**—In the far future, the investigators may discover a newly-translated sequel to *The King In Yellow*, a play called *Heir to Carcosa*. This play is not available for review in a written form, but rather has been rendered into a virtual Computer Generated Holographic (CGH) animated work.

THE KING IN YELLOW (THE PLAY)

Various Mythos authors have made attempts at creating version of this play. While details of these different attempts vary greatly, its central themes remain consistent. For our purposes I have included the summary of the play originally written by Kevin Ross in the classic 1920s scenario "Have You Seen The Yellow Sign?" from Chasoium's *The Great Old Ones*. It is this version of the play which *Ripples from Carcosa* follows most closely.

A Summary of the Play *The King In Yellow*

The work deals with the inhabitants of a decadent alien city, apparently called Yhtill, adjacent to Aldeb-aran, which is prominent in the night skies. The main characters belong to the royal family of this city (the Queen, Cassilda, Camilla, Uoht, Thale, Aldones and Alar), and most of the play deals with their squabbles over the line of succession to the throne of Yhtill.

During one such squabble the royal folk hear of a stranger in a Pallid Mask who openly wears the abhorred Yellow Sign and who, carried by winged demons, recently arrived in the city (a successful Cthulhu Mythos roll infers that these creatures are byakhee). Coinciding with the stranger's arrival are visions of an illusionary ghost-city on the opposite shore of the lake of Hali, a city whose uppermost towers appear to be obscured by one of the planet's twin moons.

The Queen and her children summon the stranger before them, and their haughty questioning of the masked being elicits much confusing allegory but few coherent answers. He claims to be an emissary of the dreaded mythical entity called The King In Yellow, or Last King. Later, at a masked ball honoring the royal family, everyone unmasks except the stranger, who reveals that his Pallid Mask is no mask at all. The offended queen and her high priest Naotalba imprison and torture the Pallid Mask, who also calls himself the Phantom of Truth, to no avail.

As the Pallid Mask dies, the true King in Yellow arrives from across the lake of Hali. Those who aren't immediately driven mad with fear notice that the dead city across the lake is no longer there. The hoary, tattered Yellow King informs them that only one city now exists on the shores of Hali, and that city is Carcosa, once known as Yhtill.

The Play ends with The King in Yellow having settled the problem of succession and with everyone fearfully awaiting their imminent demise.

Paradoxically, Hastur is referred to separately as a character and as a place.

Each reader invariably singles out a character in the play as representative of himself or herself, usually to the reader's horror when that character's doom becomes apparent.

9

Adventus Regis

BACKGROUND

The investigators begin play as a group of Roman citizens vacationing at a resort town and enjoying a relaxing escape from the pressures of life. They arrive just as a cult of Hastur is in the final stages of launching a major ritual. This dark rite takes the form of a new play which ultimately leads to madness, chaos, and the destruction of the town. The investigators must survive the insanity that grips the town, confront the core group members of the cult, and thwart their further aims. For the cult this is just the beginning, as they plan to improve the ritual, making the play more powerful, and perform it again soon to a much larger audience.

KEEPER INFORMATION

Livius Carbo was once a very successful playwright, however when his young wife died five years previously he suffered a nervous breakdown. Concerned friends and relatives suggested that he go spend some time in Herculaneum, a resort town known for its ability to soothe troubled minds. Carbo traveled there and soon made friends with a number of local artists and poets. It was through these new friends that he became involved with the Cult of Hastur.

Joining the cult, he quickly became its most gifted member. After only a year of involvement, he began dreaming of a dead city on a lakeshore, a trio of doomed nobles, and the coming of a king dressed all in yellow. Carbo recorded his dreams and eventually formed them into a play. The cult was thrilled with Carbo's creation, seeing it as a powerful tool for spreading the message of their faith. The goal of bringing this work to the stage became the chief aim of the entire cult.

For the last year the Cult of Hastur has pursued this goal vigorously. They've rented out the arena in Vestalanium to showcase the sanity-shattering drama. They have also had hundreds of bronze pendants minted, all emblazoned with the Yellow Sign, and plan to give one to each and every person attending the play.

Finding a cast was the hardest part. As slaves were commonly used as actors, the cultists purchased dozens before finding the ones right for each role. Many slaves were sold after reading only a few lines and others were driven mad before properly learning their lines. Several of these dismissed slaves were sold in Vestalanium, a few of them mentally affected by the lines they were forced to learn. Now the cult has a full cast of skilled enslaved actors, each of whom is now hopelessly insane. Their minds are filled only with the horrible play and their role within it.

The investigators arrive the night before the play is to be performed. The whole town is buzzing with excitement over the return to public life of the once-famous Carbo. Everyone is speaking about the incredible expense of the production and speculating on topic of the play. There is also much interest in the novelty of a play being performed in an arena as opposed to a traditional theater. The promise of a free gift to each attendee has everyone eager to secure a ticket to the performance.

The play is scheduled to begin as the sun begins to set. The arena will be lit by hundreds of oil lamps for the final act. This alone is enough to make people curious, as plays normally end well before sundown because of lighting. The reason for this is that Hastur cannot be summoned unless the star Aldebaran is visible above the horizon. The play is part of a ritual that the cult hopes will open the way for their god, the Great Old One Hastur, to manifest.

My
BRITISH
Ancestor

A Zap The Grandma Gap Activity Book

By Janet Hovorka & Amy Slade

How To Use This Book

This activity book is designed to help create stronger bonds in modern families by encouraging the whole family to learn about their ancestors together. Greater knowledge about family history especially strengthens and empowers youth by creating self-esteem, resilience and a greater sense of control over their lives. Studying the family's past also strengthens the relationships between living family members by creating a shared experience and core identity that no one else in the world can duplicate. Young people can take the lead to accomplish the activities in this book with their family members.

It is our hope that learning about your family's past together can be a fun and exciting adventure and that this book will help all of your family members discover joy in the quest to find out more about your ancestors .

Janet Hovorka   Amy Slade

Copyright © 2013 by Janet Hovorka and Amy Slade
All rights reserved. No part of this publication may be distributed in any printed or electronic form without written permission.

Illustrated by Bob Bonham http://www.coroflot.com/bbonham

While the authors have made every effort to provide accurate internet addresses at the time of publication, neither the authors nor the publisher assume any responsibility for changes that occur after publication. Further, neither the author nor publisher assume any responsibility for third party websites or their contents.

Published by Family ChartMasters
P.O. Box 1080 Pleasant Grove, Utah 84062
www.familychartmasters.com 801-872-4278
For more information, free downloads, quantity discounts and new resources go to
www.zapthegrandmagap.com

International Standard Book Number: 978-09888-548-2-6

Table of Contents

Introduction

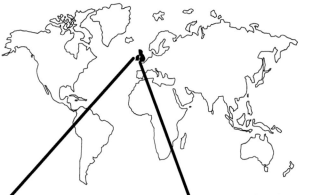

If you have British ancestors, you are really lucky. England is a beautiful country and has been important in the history of the world. England is part of the British Isles, which also includes Scotland to the North and Wales, Northern Ireland and Ireland to the West. England was the seat of the British Empire which was the largest global power in history and at one time ruled over one fifth of the world's population. As a result, England's influence has been felt in governments, languages and culture around the whole world.

If you have one British ancestor, you probably have several British ancestors. For this book, you may want to focus on the one you know the most about or the one most interesting to you, but feel free to add other pages with more information about other ancestors.

Sections of this Book

The workbook starts with pages to fill in what you know about your ancestors and instructions on where to look for more information. Then there are pages with common cultural experiences which work like puzzle pieces to help fill in what the day to day lives of your ancestors were like. The pages with references that are not specific to your family members are marked at the bottom of the page with puzzle pieces. While you may not be sure that your ancestors experienced all of the details of this cultural knowledge, these are common experiences shared by many English people in the past and very likely apply to your family.

How Am I Related To My British Ancestors?

Me

My Dad

My Mom

How many ancestors do you know?
Color the British ancestors blue.

Where Can I Find More?

Look for clues about your family history around your home.

Where does your family keep their family history pictures and documents?

_____

_____

Who do you need to ask to see them?

_____

_____

Which family members can you ask about your British ancestors?

_____

You could ask them:

☐ What do you know about our British ancestors?
☐ How am I related to them?
☐ Do you know what they looked like? Do you have any pictures?
☐ Do you know what their personalities were like?
☐ Do you have any family history keepsakes or documents? Who does?
☐ How did our family come to live where we live now?
☐ What are some stories about my British ancestors?
☐ Do you know the origin of our British surname?
☐ Are there any recipes, talents, traditions or common sayings that come from our British family history?

Check the questions you want to ask, then arrange a time to ask the questions in a family history interview.

My Ancestor's Childhood

British Ancestor's name _____

He/She was born on _____(date)
in_____(place)

His/Her parents were:

Mother's Name_____   Father's Name_____
Born _____(date)   Born _____(date)
_____(place)   _____(place)
Died _____(date)   Died _____(date)
_____(place)   _____(place)

His/her parents were married _____(date)
_____(place)

His/Her brothers and sisters were:

_____   _____

_____   _____

_____   _____

_____   _____

_____   _____

_____(7)_____

Where Can I Find Even More?

Don't fret if you don't know everything yet. Just keep looking and learning.

www.freebmd.org.uk
> An index to the birth marriage and deaths

www.nationalarchives.gov.uk
> England's archive.

www.familysearch.org
> English parish record indexes

www.genuki.org.uk
> Links to free British information by geography

www.ancestry.co.uk
> Major record groups and passenger lists

www.findmypast.co.uk
> Largest British online database company

www.thegenealogist.co.uk
> Locally built indexes for major records

www.genesreunited.co.uk
> British online family tree

www.britishorigins.com
> Miscellaneous databases from the major English genealogy society

Look for Civil Registration (Birth, Marriage and Death Certificates), Census, Church and Probate Records

My Ancestor's Adult Life

British Ancestor's Spouse's name _____

He/She was born on _____(date)
in_____(place)

They were married _____(date)
_____(place)

These ancestors are my *(circle the right number of "greats")*
great great great great great great great great great great grandparents.

Their children were:

_____   _____

_____   _____

_____   _____

_____   _____

They lived:

_____   _____

_____   _____

_____   _____

_____   _____

Me and My Ancestor

You are an important descendant of your British Ancestor.

Glue or draw a picture of yourself here.

Your Name_____

Some of your special qualities are:

_____
_____
_____
_____

You inherited some of your characteristics from your ancestors.

Draw or glue a copy of a picture of your ancestor here.

Your Ancestor's Name_____

Some qualities that you share in common:

_____
_____
_____
_____

British Schools

School for your ancestor was different from school today.

Match the experiences your ancestor might have had with modern school experiences.

School starts around 8am and finishes around 3pm.

Many different textbooks are used for different subjects.

Lunch is eaten at school.

It is very important to be on time to class.

School work is done on paper or on the computer.

School is usually mandatory until 12th grade.

Students attend Monday through Friday.

Most schools are paid for by government taxes.

Students are taught by a teacher.

Instruction is given in classrooms.

In 1870 school was mandatory until 10 years old. In 1918 until 14 years old.

School was taught from 9am to noon and from 2pm to 5pm.

Children went to school on Sunday or "Sunday School" so they could work other days of the week.

Schools were paid for by a church or a wealthy benefactor.

School work is done a sand tray or a chalkboard slate.

It was very important to be on time to class.

The Bible was the main book.

Lunch was eaten at home.

All children were taught in a central hall and small "classes" stood on a chalk semi-circle around the outer walls.

The teacher taught older students who then taught the younger children's classes.

Color the Flag

1. Color all the #1 areas red
2. Color all of the #2 areas blue

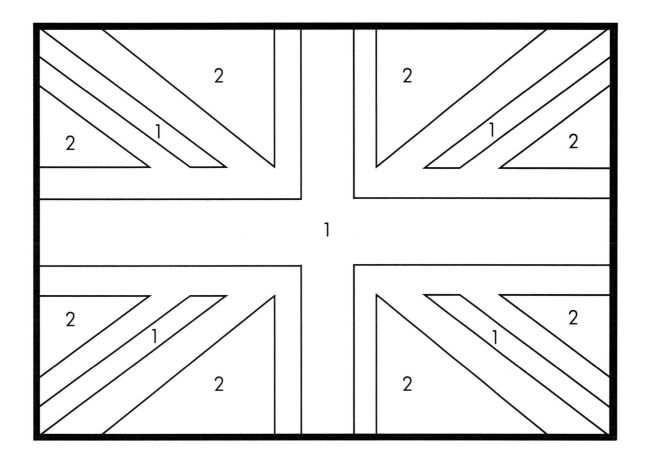

The British Flag is often called the Union Jack because of its association with the powerful British Navy. The flag or portions of it are often represented in flags of the former British colonies. The red diagonal X represents the St. Patrick's Cross, the white diagonal X represents St. Andrew's Cross, and the Red + represents St. George's cross.

Where Did They Live?

Historically, British people have lived in a variety of circumstances based on their wealth and social standing in life. The wealthy were able to live in large homes and country estates with many servants and laborers. Working class people lived in the cities and towns with smaller homes, sometimes attached to other homes, or detached from other homes on a small piece of land.

Instead of addresses, many English homes were given a name. Write the name of your ancestor's home here. _____

Unscramble each of the clue words for different types of English homes. Circle the type of home your ancestor lived in. Copy the letters in the numbered cells to other cells with the same number to reveal the hidden phrase.

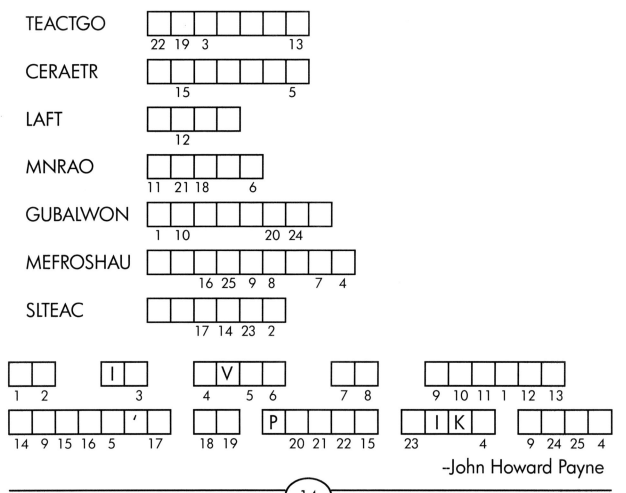

TEACTGO

CERAETR

LAFT

MNRAO

GUBALWON

MEFROSHAU

SLTEAC

--John Howard Payne

A British Landmark

If your British ancestors ever went to London, they surely would have seen the Tower of London. Built in 1070 by William the Conqueror, the castle was built to protect the King and his interests. The White Tower in the center of the castle has been the home to rulers and prisoners and has been used as a safe place to store royal jewels and weapons.

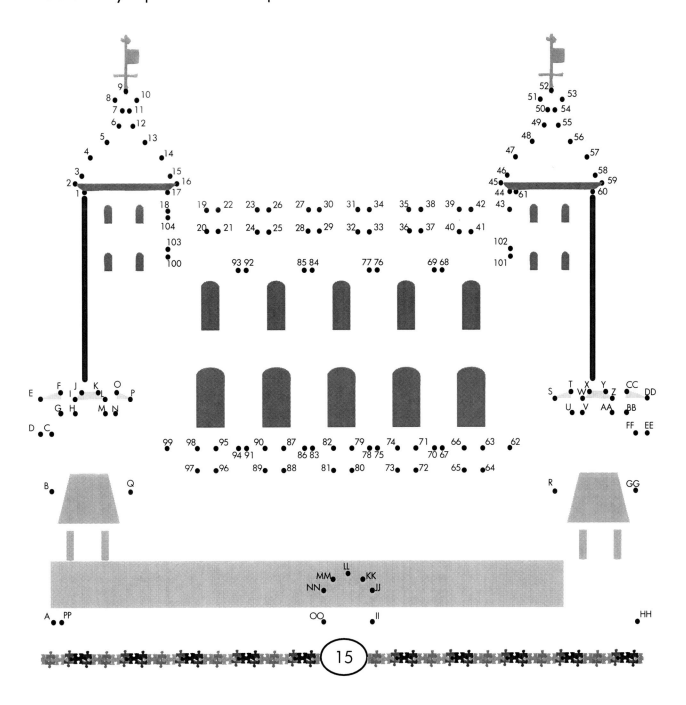

Royal Roots

If you trace your British ancestry back far enough, you may be related to a King or Queen.

Most people with British Ancestry are related to some poor people and some royalty.

Find these royal family dynasties in the maze.

```
S N A I R E V O N A H Y U Z O Y N T W S
P A V I C T O R I A N S O W I V E S I T
S N A M R O N R D Z J B K R I J N W N R
S T E N E G A T N A L P R K K O G V D A
L A N C A S T R I A N S I Q X I I R S U
N V A C Z G Z X U Q K N Z A S R S Z O T
T U D O R S P D U C G S S K P S C T R S
B I R F C M M A D S D B E Y Y W I R S F
```

Saxons
Vikings
Normans
Yorkists
Plantagenets
Lancastrians
Tudors
Stuarts
Hanoverians
Victorians
Windsors

The history of the English Kings and Queens are divided into dynasties, or families. When one family rose to power, the time that they ruled was known by the name of the family. Even the designs and artifacts from that time period are known by the name of the family. The next King or Queen was decided by their family heredity. So family relationships were very important to your British ancestors.

King   Countess   Throne
Queen   Court   Heredity
Princess   Knight   Church of England
Prince   Duty   Parliament
Duke   Honor   Buckingham Palace
Duchess   Crown   Windsor Castle
Earl   Sceptre   Magna Carta

```
S C N L M K E R E M S E Y Z S C P P X W
O Z A N L N O O K V A S N C P Q R U S I
Y S C R E N R N Z R I O E P P U I K D N
M S N H O E I I L D I B A C Q Q N U G D
X E S H U G U D E W J R R J N T C B Q S
L T Y L H R S Q Z H L I P T N I E D Y O
F N E T R F C G H I X G K K C D R T T R
B U C K I N G H A M P A L A C E I P R C
J O S X Z Q A M O V U L Z B C D X M U A
A C G Q E R E F E F O U P G E X J Z O S
S V T K E N X M X R E I R R A N L Q C T
P Q T S T M Z X G J D N E G A R K G X L
V Y S L X C R O W N H H G M B F W J N E
L G G J Y A J S R C O E I L E L C D M Q
P P I O T R U O C U S K Q Y A B D M S J
D U C H E S S R L E Y T U D E N O R H T
A T R A C A N G A M P K B Q A D D G I D
D N V T A W G S Z X U T I F B U X C R A
K V X B E C V J I R F K R N Z K P T U V
H N J Z M H I K Q S U G R E G E B P O V
```

My Ancestor's Timeline

Fill in the boxes for the times that your ancestor lived.

☐ 1666 The Great Fire of London destroyed the city.

☐ 1707 The Act of Union created the Kingdom of Great Britain from England, Wales, and Scotland

☐ About 1750 the Industrial Revolution began.

☐ 1783 The American revolution ended and America became an independent country.

☐ 1801 Ireland joined England, Scotland and Wales to become the United Kingdom of Great Britain.

☐ 1815 Britain defeated France in the Napoleonic Wars.

☐ 1825 The Stockton & Darlington railway, the world's first public passenger railway opened.

☐ 1851 Six million people visited the Great Exhibition in Hyde Park celebrating technology and design.

☐ 1914-1918 World War I

☐ 1939-1945 World War II

☐ 1921 Ireland returned to independence and the United Kingdom was again formed from England, Scotland and Wales.

Do You Know English?

Some of the words your ancestors used were unique to their British home.

Across
4. Policeman
6. Cookie
7. Apartment
8. Jail
9. Goodbye
Down
1. Garbage
2. Two Weeks
3. Surprised
5. Sweater
9. French Fries

My Ancestor's Home

England is part of the
British Isles
which also includes
Ireland, Northern
Ireland, Scotland,
and Wales.

*Label and draw a
red star near where your
ancestor lived.*

Scotland

Northern
Ireland

Ireland

Wales

England

*Fill in the blanks for these cities:
Bristol, Edinburgh, Belfast,
Manchester, London, Plymouth,
Bradford, Southampton,
Leeds, Liverpool, Dublin,
Glasgow, Cardiff*

My Ancestor's Journeys

How did your family get to where you are now? Did your ancestor visit any other countries? Who moved to the place you live today?

British Fairy Tale

Your ancestor may have heard this story when they were tucked in for bed at night.

Cap O' Rushes

Once upon a time there was a King who had three daughters. One day he decided to find out how much each daughter loved him. So he asked each girl, "How much do you love me, my dears?"

"Why, as I love my life." said the first. "That is good." said the King.

"Why, better than all the world." answered the second. "That is good." said the King.

"Why, I love you as fresh meat loves salt." answered the youngest daughter. The King was angry with this answer. "You don't love me at all!" he cried and drove her from the kingdom.

The youngest daughter collected a few dresses from her room and travelled far from her home. When she came to a fen (swamp) outside of a city in a neighboring kingdom, she made a cloak with a hood out of rushes (grasses that grow in swampy areas) to wear over her fine clothing. She then went into the city to the greatest house, the King's house.

"I have nowhere to go, and no family here. I will do any sort of work. Do you need a maid?" she asked of the cook.

"Well, if you would like to wash the pots and keep the fires up you may stay here." the cook said. So she stayed. She washed the pots and saucepans and plates. She cleaned and stoked the fire for the cook. She would tell no one her name, so everyone began to call her "Cap-o'-Rushes" because of her cloak and hood made from rushes.

One day, months later, there was to be a great dance held at the King's household. All the servants wanted to go see all the fine people at the ball. Cap-o'-Rushes told the cook she was too tired to go, but when everyone else was gone she cleaned up and changed out of her cloak of rushes to one of her fine dresses, and snuck into the grand hall. The

Prince fell in love with her at their first dance and would only dance with her the whole evening. At the end of the night, Cap-o'-Rushes slipped away to the kitchens, changed into her cloak of rushes, and was asleep before all the servants returned.

The next morning the servants could only talk about the lovely girl that danced with the prince all evening. "There will be another dance tonight, Cap-o'-Rushes. You can see her then." But come that evening, Cap-o'-Rushes again said that she was too tired. Everyone left and she cleaned up, changed from her cloak of rushes to a gown, and went to the ball. Again the prince would only dance with her the whole evening, falling more in love with her at every moment. Cap-o'-Rushes slipped away that evening at the end of the ball, returning to the kitchens and changing before everyone returned.

The next day the servants told her again of the beautiful girl dancing with the prince. "No one knows who she is. But tonight there will be another night of dancing and you will get to see her then." they told her. That evening, all happened as the two nights before. Cap-o'-Rushes again stated that she was too tired, waiting to clean up and change after everyone left. She returned to the grand hall to dance with the prince one more evening.

The prince danced with no one else all evening. As they were dancing he placed a gold ring onto her finger. When the final song was played, the prince bowed to Cap-o'-Rushes and she returned to the kitchens just as before. This time, she only had time to put her cloak of rushes over her fine dress before the cook returned.

"I need you to make some gruel for the prince tonight. He is dying for the love of a lady." As Cap-o'-Rushes worked, the gold ring slipped off her finger and into the gruel. The prince ate and found the ring at the bottom of the bowl.

He called the cook up and asked, "Who made this gruel?"

"Why, only Cap-o'-Rushes." the cook answered.

"Bring Cap-o'-Rushes to me." the prince requested. So Cap-o'-Rushes came.

"Did you make my gruel?" the prince asked.

"Yes I did." she said.

"Where did you get this ring?" the prince asked, holding the ring up for her to see.

"From him that gave it to me." she answered.

"Who are you, then?" he asked.

"Let me show you." She then removed her cloak of rushes to show the fine dress underneath, revealing that she was the lovely girl the prince had fallen in love with.

They were to be married, and many people were invited, including Cap-o'-Rushes father, although she did not reveal to him who she was. Cap-o'-Rushes requested that the cook prepare all the dinners for guests, except the dish for her father. She prepared that dinner herself, with no salt on the meat. The wedding day came, and the dinner was prepared. Cap-o'-Rushes, now the new princess, served her father his dinner, but after one bite, the meat was so tasteless that he could not eat it.

"What is the matter?" she asked her father.

"Oh, I had a daughter that I turned away because I thought she didn't love me. But now I see that she loved me best of all. Now I fear that she is dead." the King explained.

"No, father, she is here!" Cap-o'-Rushes hugged her father and so they were all happy ever after.

British Food

A traditional English desert generally consisted of a pudding: a moist cake including fruit, topped with a cream sauce. Sticky Toffee Pudding is a modern take on a British classic that many children love today.

Sticky Toffee Pudding -- 8 servings

CAKE
4 Tbs butter, softened
3/4 cup dark brown sugar
1 egg
1 cup all-purpose flour
1/2 tsp baking powder
1/2 tsp baking soda
1 cup (plus) boiling water
3/4 cup pitted dates
1 tsp vanilla extract

SAUCE
3/4 cup brown sugar
6 Tbs butter
1/2 cup cream

Preheat oven to 350. Get the water boiling on the stove and chop the dates pretty finely. Pour 1 cup boiling water over the dates. Stir in the baking powder, soda and vanilla. Let soak for about 5 minutes or so. While the dates soak, in a separate bowl cream the butter and sugar together. Add the egg and beat until smooth. Mix in the flour. Add the date mixture and mix well. Pour into 8x8 (or similar size) greased baking dish and bake for 30-40 minutes. Toothpick should come out clean when done. When cake is about done, melt butter for sauce in small pan. Add brown sugar and cream and bring to a boil. Boil for 2-3 minutes until texture is smooth and velvety. Serve cake warm with warm sauce poured over it. Top with a dollop of whipped cream if desired.

Holidays

Boxing Day is a British public holiday celebrated on 26th of December, the day after Christmas Day. Traditionally, Boxing Day was a day for giving money and goods to the less fortunate. Affluent British family members gathered and exchanged gifts with each other on Christmas, but the day after their attention was turned to helping people of the lower classes. They boxed up food, goods and money to give as presents for their servants and working class people.

How many boxes are in this stack to give to the poor?

You can celebrate Boxing Day any day of the year. Do you have any nice toys that you don't use anymore or well kept clothes that don't fit? You can box them up for a charity that will share them with kids in need.

Music

"Twinkle Twinkle Little Star" is a traditional British children's song. In 1806, Jane Taylor wrote the poem Twinkle Twinkle Little Star. It is sung to the French tune "Ah! vous dirai-je, Maman" which was first seen in print in 1761, but made famous by Mozart's variations in 1781-2.

Twinkle Twinkle Little Star

Jane Taylor 1806   French Tune "Ah! vous dirai-je, Maman"

Twinkle, twinkle, little star,
How I wonder what you are.
Up above the world so high,
Like a diamond in the sky.

When the blazing sun is gone
When he nothing shines upon,
Then you show your little light,
Twinkle, twinkle, all the night.

Then the traveller in the dark,
Thanks you for your tiny spark,
He could not see which way to go,
If you did not twinkle so.

In the dark blue sky you keep,
And often through my curtains peep.
For you never shut your eye,
'Till the sun is in the sky.

As your bright and tiny spark,
Lights the traveller in the dark,
Though I know not what you are.
Twinkle, twinkle little star.

Twinkle, twinkle little star
How I wonder what you are.
Up above the world so high.
Like a diamond in the sky.

Twinkle, twinkle, little star. How I wonder what you are.

Royal Mail

The Royal Mail postal service was established in 1516 by King Henry VIII and has been an important part of the success of the British businesses and the British Empire. Before telephones or the internet, it also allowed distant friends and family members to communicate easily and effectively. The letter carrier's daily visit brought news, invitations, and excitement to our ancestors.

Letters were often sealed with melted wax to secure that they were not read until the recipient opened them. Family crests were made into embossed seals that were pushed into the wax to identify the sender. Draw your family crest here in the wax on this envelope, or design a new one. You can create your own wax seal by carving the crest into a piece of wood, or a potato and then practice sealing an envelope with melted candle wax.

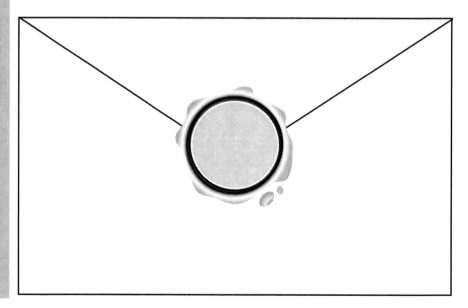

A Letter to My Ancestor

What would you say to your ancestor if you could talk to them today?

Dear _____

Sincerely,

_____

Oh Yeah? Prove It.

Documents prove what happened in the past. What documents have come from your British family's life that will prove to someone in the future that they were alive?

Paste an envelope here.
Make copies of documents from your ancestor's life, like
letters, civil registration, census, church and probate records and pictures.
Store your own copies of these documents in this envelope.
Original copies of important items should be kept in a very safe place.

Invite The Family to Tea

The English tradition of having tea began in the early 1800s. Women would get together to socialize while the men were working. At that time tea was very expensive and precious. It was a sign of wealth and status if you were able to serve tea to friends and acquaintances. Later, taxes on tea were reduced and the custom of afternoon tea spread to more people, becoming a cultural tradition.

You Are Invited To A

Family Tea Party

♥♥♥♥♥♥♥♥♥♥♥♥♥♥♥♥♥♥♥

Place:

Time:

Please RSVP to:

Tea Party Etiquette

Invite your mother, father, grandmother, grandfather or other older relative or friend to tea! You can invite them with an invitation in the mail like the one above—telling your special guest the date and time of your tea party. Your special guest can even help you prepare for your tea party.

You will be the host or hostess. The host or hostess always pours the tea. Sugar and cream are generally added to tea, depending on the preferences of the person drinking it. Sugar would either be kept in a small container to be spooned out or was cubed, which generally required small tongs to place sugar in the tea. Cream would be poured from a small pitcher, which was part of the tea set. Special small spoons are used to measure out sugar and stir the tea, called tea spoons. You may ask your guest if they would like "one lump or two" to see if they want one or two cubes or spoonfuls of sugar.

Prepare for Tea:

Tea can be served inside or outside. If the day is nice, you can set up a table for tea in the shade of a tree for a picnic tea party.

Cover your table with a pretty cloth, or with a family quilt. Create a centerpiece using old family photos or heirlooms—make sure to ask permission to use items that are fragile. Use copies of photographs of your parents, grandparents, and other ancestors. You can add flowers in a vase, and even have placemats made from lace or doilies.

Set out your tea set. A tea set usually includes a tea pot, a bowl for sugar, a pitcher for cream and tea cups, saucers and plates. If you do not have cups and saucers to use, perhaps go to a local thrift shop to buy some inexpensive but fancy looking china to set your table with.

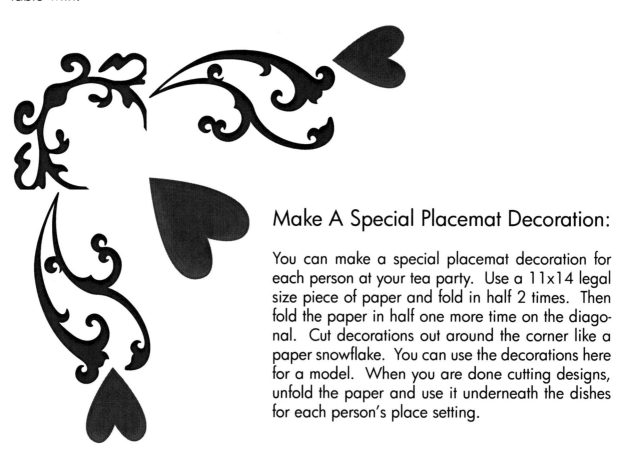

Make A Special Placemat Decoration:

You can make a special placemat decoration for each person at your tea party. Use a 11x14 legal size piece of paper and fold in half 2 times. Then fold the paper in half one more time on the diagonal. Cut decorations out around the corner like a paper snowflake. You can use the decorations here for a model. When you are done cutting designs, unfold the paper and use it underneath the dishes for each person's place setting.

How to Make a Cup of Tea:

Tea time does not mean you must serve tea. Any drink you want can be served, juice, lemonade, or even hot chocolate. You can use herbal teas too. Try using different flavors of tea at different parties. Making tea is easy, especially if you have an adult to help you.

- Fill a kettle with water and set on stove to boil

- Warm teapot by running hot water from the faucet into the teapot. Pour out the faucet water and place teabags into the teapot. Two to three bags is enough for four people.

- When water in kettle comes to a boil, remove from heat and let rest for a minute. Then pour water from the kettle into the teapot.

- After about five minutes, your tea will be ready to serve!

A Tea Superstition:
To spill a little tea while making it is lucky

Spiced Tea

2 cups dry powdered fruit drink and sugar according to package.
½ cup red hot candies
1 teaspoon cinnamon
½ teaspoon cloves

Stir together all ingredients and keep in a sealed container. When using mix for tea, use a heaping tablespoon for each cup of hot water and stir well.

Raisin Jam Sandwiches

Raisin Bread
Cream Cheese
Fruit Jam or Jelly

Spread thin layer of fruit jam or jelly over one bread slice. Spread cream cheese layer over another bread slice and close sandwich. Cut off crusts and cut into desired shapes.

Teatime Treats

A proper tea includes little sandwiches and treats to go with tea. You can also serve small cookies and cakes for sweet treats. Sandwiches usually have crusts cut off, and are cut into small shapes: like squares, triangles, or you can even use cookie cutters to cut fun shapes. You can serve any kind of sandwich you wish, but here are a few ideas.

Cucumber Sandwiches

Cucumbers
White Bread
Cream Cheese
Salt

Peel cucumbers and cut into thin slices. Sprinkle salt over the sliced cucumbers. Spread cream cheese layer over bread slices and place cucumbers on top. Close sandwiches and cut off crusts, then cut into squares or other desired shapes.

Tea Party Activities

Tea time is more than just drinking tea and eating treats; it is about getting to know more about the people you are with. Whether your special guest is a mother or grandmother or another adult relative or friend, you can spend some time playing games or telling stories. Some ideas for your tea party are:

• Storytelling Time: Ask your special guest about their life. What was their favorite house they grew up in? Who was their best teacher? Who was their best friend when they were your age? What did they want to be when they were growing up? You can even ask for advice about things that are going on in your life. When you finish, they can ask you about your life and favorite things.

• Family Photographs and Heirlooms: Look at family photos, scrapbooks, and heirlooms and talk about them. Perhaps your guest knows stories about the photographs and items and will tell you about them.

• Favorite Games, Songs, and Dances: Share your favorite game, song, or dance with your guest. Then let them share their favorite with you. You can play the game together, sing your favorite song, and even dance together.

• Paper Dolls: Color and cut out the paper dolls from this book, on pages 37-45. Use them to tell stories from your ancestor's life.

Who wouldn't like to drink afternoon tea

Out in the garden just like me

With the song of a bird, and the hum of a bee,

And the sunflowers looking, all eyes to see.

Games and Toys

Marbles

The point of the game of marbles is to knock marbles out of a ring. A large ring is drawn on a level surface, with marbles placed in a cross in the middle of the ring. The marbles are about three inches apart.

Each player uses a larger marble, called a shooter, to try to knock a marble outside of the ring. The first player uses the shooter to knock a marble out of the ring. If the shooter remains inside the ring after making contact with a marble, the player shoots from that place. If the shooter stops rolling outside of the ring after making contact with a marble, the player may shoot from any side of the circle. If the shooter does not make contact with any marble, the player is finished with their turn and the next player tries to knock marbles out of the ring. The winner is the player who knocks the most marbles out of the ring.

Duck Duck Goose

This is a game still popular today. Duck Duck Goose is a game with one person who is It, and the rest of the players sit in a circle. It goes around the circle, tapping all the players' heads as they pass calling out "Duck". When It taps a player and calls out "Goose", It begins to run around the circle with Goose chasing It. If Goose taps It, the player remains It and begins again. If It is able to make it around the circle and sit in the Goose's place in the circle, then the Goose becomes It and the game begins again.

Post Office

This game has many variants today. Each player picks a city name, like London, Preston, or Liverpool. Players sit in a circle with one person who is It standing in the middle of the circle of players. It calls out a postal route, like "London to Manchester". The players who have chosen London and Manchester must switch seats in the circle. It tries to sit in one of the players seats before they are able to switch. Whoever is left without a seat is It, and the game continues with It calling out different postal routes.

Paper Dolls

Color and cut out these paper dolls. You can play with them and use them to tell your family members stories about your ancestors.

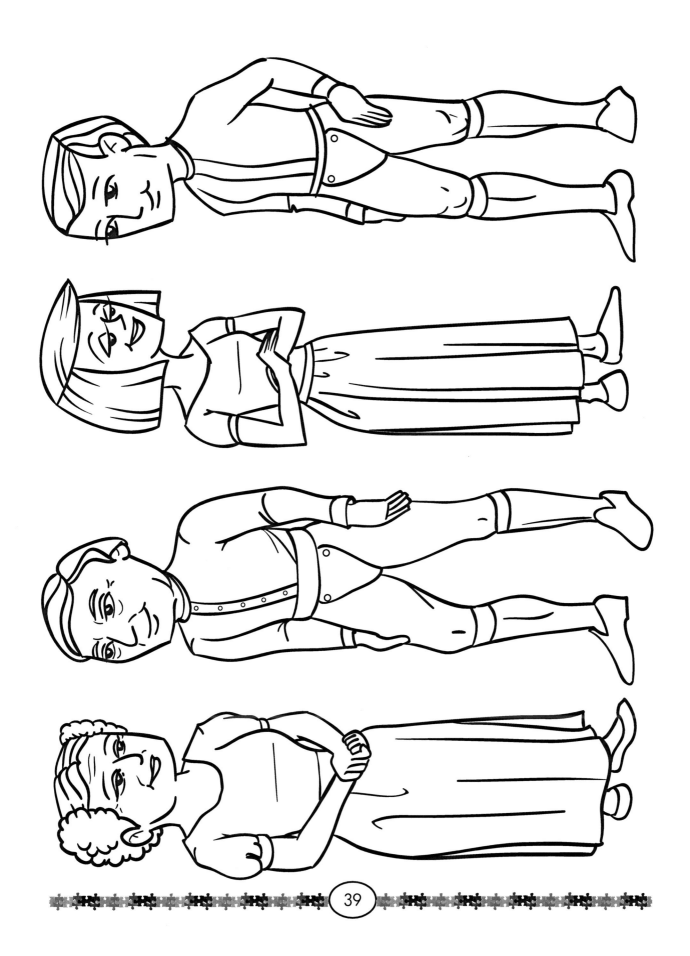

Paper Doll Clothes

Modern and superhero clothing can be downloaded at www.zapthegrandmagap.com

Zap The Grandma Gap
Certificate of Completion

_____

has been able to bridge the gap and learn about

_____

their British ancestor.

Thanks to _____

for helping complete the activities and research in this workbook.

_____

Date

Answers

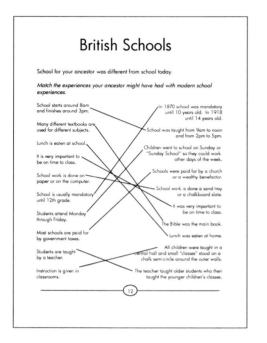

British Schools

School for your ancestor was different from school today.

Match the experiences your ancestor might have had with modern school experiences.

School starts around 8am and finishes around 3pm.

Many different textbooks are used for different subjects.

Lunch is eaten at school.

It is very important to be on time to class.

School work is done on paper or on the computer.

School is usually mandatory until 12th grade.

Students attend Monday through Friday.

Most schools are paid for by government taxes.

Students are taught by a teacher.

Instruction is given in classrooms.

In 1870 school was mandatory until 10 years old. In 1918 until 14 years old.

School was taught from 9am to noon and from 2pm to 5pm.

Children went to school on Sunday or "Sunday School" so they could work other days of the week.

Schools were paid for by a church or a wealthy benefactor.

School work is done on a sand tray or a chalkboard slate.

It was very important to be on time to class.

The Bible was the main book.

Lunch was eaten at home.

All children were taught in a central hall and small "classes" stood on a chalk semi-circle around the outer walls.

The teacher taught older students who then taught the younger children's classes.

12

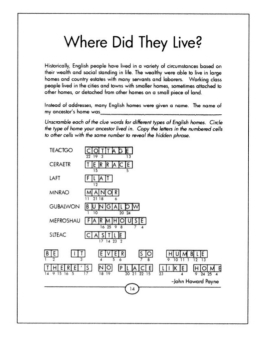

Where Did They Live?

Historically, English people have lived in a variety of circumstances based on their wealth and social standing in life. The wealthy were able to live in large homes and country estates with many servants and laborers. Working class people lived in the cities and towns with smaller homes, sometimes attached to other homes, or detached from other homes on a small piece of land.

Instead of addresses, many English homes were given a name. The name of my ancestor's home was_____

Unscramble each of the clue words for different types of English homes. Circle the type of home your ancestor lived in. Copy the letters in the numbered cells to other cells with the same number to reveal the hidden phrase.

TEACTGO — C O T T A G E
CERAETR — T E R R A C E
LAFT — F L A T
MNRAO — M A N O R
GUBALWON — B U N G A L O W
MEFROSHAU — F A R M H O U S E
SLTEAC — C A S T L E

BE IT EVER SO HUMBLE THERE'S NO PLACE LIKE HOME

–John Howard Payne

14

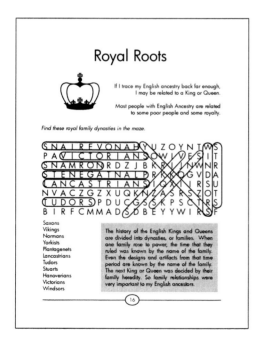

Royal Roots

If I trace my English ancestry back far enough, I may be related to a King or Queen.

Most people with English Ancestry are related to some poor people and some royalty.

Find these royal family dynasties in the maze.

Saxons
Vikings
Normans
Yorkists
Plantagenets
Lancastrians
Tudors
Stuarts
Hanoverians
Victorians
Windsors

The history of the English Kings and Queens are divided into dynasties, or families. When one family rose to power, the time that they ruled was known by the name of the family. Even the designs and artifacts from that time period are known by the name of the family. The next King or Queen was decided by their family heredity. So family relationships were very important to my English ancestors.

16

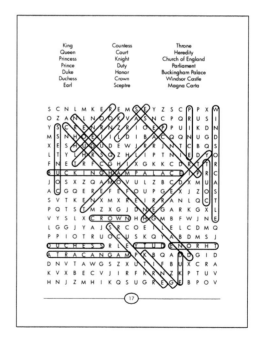

King
Queen
Princess
Prince
Duke
Duchess
Earl

Countess
Court
Knight
Duty
Honor
Crown
Sceptre

Throne
Heredity
Church of England
Parliament
Buckingham Palace
Windsor Castle
Magna Carta

17

Answers

Do You Know English?

Some of the words my ancestors used were unique to their English homeland.

Across
4. Policeman
6. Cookie
7. Apartment
8. Jail
9. Goodbye

Down
1. Garbage
2. Two Weeks
3. Surprised
5. Sweater
9. French Fries

19

My Ancestor's Home

England is part of the British Isles which also include Ireland, Northern Ireland, Scotland, and Wales.

Label and draw a red star near where your ancestor lived.

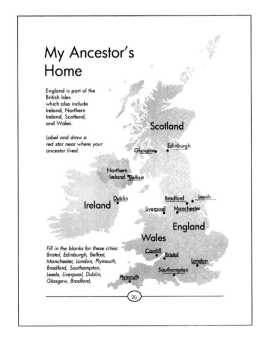

Fill in the blanks for these cities:
Bristol, Edinburgh, Belfast, Manchester, London, Plymouth, Bradford, Southampton, Leeds, Liverpool, Dublin, Glasgow, Bradford,

20

My Ancestor's Journeys

How did your family get to where you are now? Did your ancestor visit any other countries? Who moved to the country you live in today?

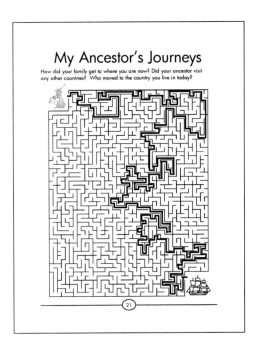

21

Holidays

Boxing Day is a English public holiday celebrated on 26th of December, the day after Christmas Day. Traditionally, Boxing Day was a day for giving money and goods to the less fortunate. Affluent English family members gathered and exchanged gifts with each other on Christmas, but the day after their attention was turned to helping people of the lower classes. They boxed up food, goods and money to give as presents for their servants and working class people.

How many boxes are in this stack to give to the poor?

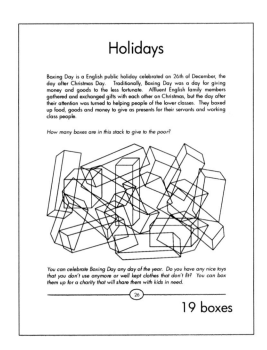

You can celebrate Boxing Day any day of the year. Do you have any nice toys that you don't use anymore or well kept clothes that don't fit? You can box them up for a charity that will share them with kids in need.

26

19 boxes

Further Resources

See also the Genealogy Resources on page 8.
For more information about British culture and history:

www.horrible-histories.co.uk
   The website for the fun British TV show about history. Check out Horrible Histories on YouTube too.
www.visitengland.com
   The English Tourism Website. A great place to learn about the geography, history and culture of England.
www.royal.gov.uk
   The official website of the British Monarchy. Learn about the history of the Royal Family and their royal residences.
www.visitlondon.com
   The London Tourism Website. Check out historical and modern London and start planning a trip.
www.nationaltrust.org.uk
   Explore the National Trust which cares for England's historical sites.
www.bbc.co.uk
   Check out the British Broadcasting Company for news and culture.

For British fiction reading, you might want to try out works by:

Arthur Conan Doyle
Jane Austen
William Shakespeare
Charles Dickens
Neil Gaiman
Jasper Fforde
P. L. Travers
A. A. Milne
J.K. Rowling
Lewis Carroll
C.S. Lewis
Lucy M. Boston

More Resources

References and Suggested Readings:

May, Trevor. *The Victorian Schoolroom.* Shire Publications: Oxford UK, 2011.

Peters, Beryl. *The Etiquette of an English Tea.* Copper Beech Publishing: East Grinstead, England, 1995.

Barnes, Emilie. *Let's Have a Tea Party!* Harvest House Publishers: Eugene OR, 1997.

Sacks, Janet. *Victorian Childhood.* Shire Publications: Oxford UK, 2011.

Parker, Michael St. John. *Life in Victorian England.* Pitkin Publishing: Hampshire UK, 2010.

MacDonald, Fiona. *You Wouldn't Want To Be A Victorian Servant!* Scholastic, New York, 2006.

Malam, John. *You Wouldn't Want To Be A Victorian Mill Worker!* Scholastic, New York, 2007.

Take a look at **zapthegrandmagap.com** for more ideas and free downloads to explore your family history and make it fun for all ages:

•Get the book *Zap The Grandma Gap: Connect to Your Family By Connecting The To Their Family History* and it's companion *Power Up Workbook* for 100s of easy family history ideas.
•Sign up on the website for the weekly newsletter with one simple idea each week to create stronger bonds in your family.

CPSIA information can be obtained at www.ICGtesting.com
Printed in the USA
LVOW09s2102040914

402463LV00026B/868/P

9 780988 854826